"*Knowing Jesse* is Leone's heartbreaking, uplifting, occasionally over-heated, but never, ever saccharine account of three brave people fighting for their humanity ... At its core, *Knowing Jesse* is about the Coopers' battle to establish in the minds of others who their child actually was and who, with help, he ultimately could become. Their objective never changed: to prove that Jesse was something far greater than a crumpled, spastic little boy."   —*Los Angeles Times*

"This book will break your heart. This book will make you angry. It will make you laugh and cry and cheer. But mostly, this book will lift you up."
                              —Ann Hood, author of *Comfort*

"A mother's passion-filled memoir of her fight to give her disabled son the life he deserved ... Love for her son and rage at those who did not see him as worthwhile permeate the narrative, which surprises with its humor and frankness ... Leone's character sketches are deft and humorous, and included throughout are selections of Jesse's poetry and photographs of the boy with family and friends, attesting to a life that, though short and often painful, was filled with accomplishment, love, and joy. Heartwarming."   —*Kirkus Reviews*

"Funny, fierce, and illuminating ... You have to get this."
                                              —*Boston Herald*

"The stark beauty of this memoir hit me the moment I began. Marianne Leone's narrative, written with an unrelenting immediacy, yanked me into her world ... [*Knowing Jesse*] gave me one of the greatest gifts of my reading life ... This book lives on my 'read again and again' shelf."   —*HuffPost*

"In prose so full of life and love and rage and grace it will fill the room where you read this book, Marianne Leone tells the story of her son Jesse, a boy with cerebral palsy, a beautiful boy—brave, smart, funny, and determined to live his life as part of society, not segregated from it. Armed with a ferocious love, his parents set out to make sure Jesse has that chance ... This is a love story, and a family story, and at its heart is the boy. Jesse died young, but he lives in these pages. I am grateful to have met him here."   —Abigail Thomas, author of *A Three Dog Life*

"This book made me laugh and cry and then laugh again until I was crying with laughter ... This kid's journey is one of a kind and so is this book. Do yourself a favor: buy it, read it, and when you are done—read it again."
                    —Denis Leary, author of *Why We Suck*

"*Knowing Jesse* is an incandescent memoir, glowing with a mother's love for her disabled son, and fueled by her righteous anger at a system that failed time and time again to acknowledge his humanity. Marianne Leone tells her family's story with fierce honesty and unexpected humor, illuminating not only the challenges of Jesse's life, but the courage with which he faced them, and the joy he brought to the people who were lucky enough to know him."
                    —Tom Perrotta, author of *Tracy Flick Can't Win*

"*Knowing Jesse* is an important book for any parent with a severely disabled child to read, and maybe an even more important one for the rest of us blessed with kids we think of as 'normal.' No parent should ever have to struggle the way the Coopers did for their beloved son, not here or anywhere. Their story forces us to imagine ourselves in their shoes and to face the hard question of whose responsibility it is to speak for children who cannot speak for themselves."
                    —Richard Russo, author of *Marriage Story: An American Memoir*